The more gorgeous the country, the better elk seem to like it. So do we humans. Elk country is God's country for sure, but it's not nearly as boundless as it feels. Every day across the West another 5,000 acres of prime habitat is bulldozed and lost forever to development. The Rocky Mountain Elk Foundation has spent 25 years fighting to protect the priceless places that are bread and butter to America's wapiti.

Along the way we've conserved more than 5.5 million acres of prime habitat and opened 500,000 acres of previously off-limits country to the public for everyone to enjoy.

One of our strengths has been our ability to make friends and build partnerships. We work shoulder to shoulder with private landowners, federal and state agencies and many other groups to enhance habitat through prescribed fires, noxious weed treatments, seedings and a dozen other methods to assure that habitat for elk is as fertile as it can be.

But this work is just beginning. Houses, roads and box stores are gobbling open space faster than at any time in history. As land values skyrocket, ranching and farming families are pressured to sell what are often a region's most productive and beautiful lands. When we lose these places, both wildlife and our way of life suffer.

If you love elk and elk country, help make a difference. Join the Elk Foundation today and help ensure a future for elk, other wildlife and our grandchildren.

MAKE A DIFFERENCE FOR THE FUTURE OF ELK COUNTRY.

To join please call (800) CALL-ELK *or visit* www.elkfoundation.org.

inset photo by Paul Queneau
background photo by Becky Blankenship/Images on the Wildside

JANUARY

Still exhausted from the rut, bulls rely heavily on their fat reserves as winter snow deepens. Outlasting the cold until spring's greenup is a balancing act, and the tipping point is healthy and abundant habitat.

SUNDAY	MONDAY	TUESDAY	WEDNESDAY	THURSDAY	FRIDAY	SATURDAY

DECEMBER 2009
       1 2 3 4
5 6 7 8 9 10 11
12 13 14 15 16 17 18
19 20 21 22 23 24 25
26 27 28 29 30 31
	FEBRUARY 2010
	    1 2 3 4 5 6
	7 8 9 10 11 12 13
	14 15 16 17 18 19 20
	21 22 23 24 25 26 27
	28
					NEW YEAR'S DAY 1	2

3	4	5	6	7 ◐ LAST QUARTER	8	9
10	11	12	13	14	15 ● NEW MOON	16
17	18 MARTIN LUTHER KING JR. DAY	19	20	21	22	23 ◑ FIRST QUARTER
24	25	26	27	28	29	30 ○ FULL MOON
31						

5705 Grant Creek Road
Missoula, Montana 59808
800-CALL ELK
www.elkfoundation.org

Lying hard against Montana's Rocky Mountain Front, it's not hard to see why folks would love to plant trophy homes along Dupuyer Creek. For now, this country remains both vital home and travel corridor for elk, moose, deer, grizzlies, wolverines, and more. Thanks to a conservation easement donated to the Elk Foundation, 2,900 acres of it will forever be protected.

TOP PHOTO © DONALDMJONES.COM
BOTTOM PHOTO © PAUL N. QUENEAU

FEBRUARY

Bull elk hold onto their antlers through the winter, a strategy biologists believe helps maintain the established social structure after bulls band back together following the rut—sometimes en masse.

SUNDAY	MONDAY	TUESDAY	WEDNESDAY	THURSDAY	FRIDAY	SATURDAY
	1	2 GROUNDHOG DAY	3	4	5 ◐ LAST QUARTER	6
7	8	9	10	11	12	13 ● NEW MOON
14 VALENTINE'S DAY	15 PRESIDENTS' DAY	16	17 ASH WEDNESDAY	18	19	20
21 ◑ FIRST QUARTER	22	23	24	25	26	27
28 ○ FULL MOON						

JANUARY 2010

					1	2
3	4	5	6	7	8	9
10	11	12	13	14	15	16
17	18	19	20	21	22	23
24	25	26	27	28	29	30
31						

MARCH 2010

	1	2	3	4	5	6
7	8	9	10	11	12	13
14	15	16	17	18	19	20
21	22	23	24	25	26	27
28	29	30	31			

5705 Grant Creek Road
Missoula, Montana 59808
800-CALL ELK
www.elkfoundation.org

Researchers swooped down in a helicopter to adorn thirty cow elk in Wyoming's Absa-roka Range with GPS collars as part of an Elk Foundation–sponsored study of habitat use, migration patterns, and predation. Biologists hope this will get them up to speed on a herd that has seen a multitude of changes in the past two hundred years.

TOP PHOTO © HENRY HOLDSWORTH
BOTTOM PHOTO © ELK FOUNDATION

MARCH

"It is a fragile thing, this natural wilderness, consisting of the material for poetry and art and vigorous, clean living. It is easily degraded or destroyed by heedless men."
—Olaus Murie, The Elk of North America

SUNDAY	MONDAY	TUESDAY	WEDNESDAY	THURSDAY	FRIDAY	SATURDAY
	1	2	3	4	5	6
7 ◐ LAST QUARTER	8	9	10	11	12	13
DAYLIGHT SAVING TIME BEGINS — 14	15 ● NEW MOON	16	ST. PATRICK'S DAY — 17	18	19	SPRING EQUINOX — 20
21	22	23 ◑ FIRST QUARTER	24	25	26 FEBRUARY 2010 1 2 3 4 5 6 7 8 9 10 11 12 13 14 15 16 17 18 19 20 21 22 23 24 25 26 27 28	27 APRIL 2010 1 2 3 4 5 6 7 8 9 10 11 12 13 14 15 16 17 18 19 20 21 22 23 24 25 26 27 28 29 30
28	PASSOVER BEGINS AT SUNDOWN — 29 ○ FULL MOON	30	31			

5705 Grant Creek Road
Missoula, Montana 59808
800-CALL ELK
www.elkfoundation.org

Vital to most ecosystems across the West, fire thins forests and allows nutrient-rich grasses and forbs to flourish. Forests become choked and sickly when we suppress wildfire. In such a state, they're far less valuable for wildlife and far more prone to catastrophic wildfire. To restore fire to this Arizona forest, the Elk Foundation helped fund a prescribed burn on 1,900 acres.

TOP PHOTO © CLIFF BEITTEL
BOTTOM PHOTO © ELK FOUNDATION

APRIL

Yellowstone's Electric Peak overlooks some of the grandest elk country our continent has to offer—and what once was one of the last wild holdouts of the wapiti as they approached extinction in the late 1800s. Yellowstone then served as the "calving grounds of the nation," an invaluable source of the animals that rekindled wiped-out herds across America.

SUNDAY	MONDAY	TUESDAY	WEDNESDAY	THURSDAY	FRIDAY	SATURDAY

MARCH 2010
  1 2 3 4 5 6
 7 8 9 10 11 12 13
14 15 16 17 18 19 20
21 22 23 24 25 26 27
28 29 30 31
	MAY 2010
	                  1
	 2 3 4 5 6 7 8
	 9 10 11 12 13 14 15
	16 17 18 19 20 21 22
	23 24 25 26 27 28 29
	30 31
				APRIL FOOL'S DAY **1**	GOOD FRIDAY **2**	**3**

EASTER **4**	**5**	**6** ◐ LAST QUARTER	**7**	**8**	**9**	**10**
11	**12**	**13**	**14** ● NEW MOON	TAX DAY **15**	**16**	**17**
18	**19**	**20**	**21** ◐ FIRST QUARTER	EARTH DAY **22**	**23**	**24**
25	**26**	**27**	**28** ○ FULL MOON	**29**	**30**	

5705 Grant Creek Road
Missoula, Montana 59808
800-CALL ELK
www.elkfoundation.org

Montana's Bundy Bridge fire seared 90,000 acres, and some areas were so badly blistered that nothing sprouted the following spring. Working around April's spotty snow schedule, Elk Foundation volunteers helped plant 3,750 shrub seedlings of six different native species across 250 ashen acres, punctuating the black with exclamation points of green.

Top Photo © Ken Archer
Bottom Photo © Elk Foundation

MAY

A bull elk will literally strip the calcium from its bones as it pours energy into antler growth—sprouting as much as an inch a day, a growth rate equal to the most aggressive jungle plants.

SUNDAY	MONDAY	TUESDAY	WEDNESDAY	THURSDAY	FRIDAY	SATURDAY

APRIL 2010
               1 2 3
4 5 6 7 8 9 10
11 12 13 14 15 16 17
18 19 20 21 22 23 24
25 26 27 28 29 30
	JUNE 2010
	      1 2 3 4 5
	6 7 8 9 10 11 12
	13 14 15 16 17 18 19
	20 21 22 23 24 25 26
	27 28 29 30
						1

2	3	4	CINCO DE MAYO 5	6 ◐ LAST QUARTER	7	8
MOTHER'S DAY 9	10	11	12	13 ● NEW MOON	14	ARMED FORCES DAY 15
16	17	18	19	20 ◑ FIRST QUARTER	21	22
23	24	VICTORIA DAY (CANADA) 25	26	27 ○ FULL MOON	28	29
30	MEMORIAL DAY 31					

5705 Grant Creek Road
Missoula, Montana 59808
800-CALL ELK
www.elkfoundation.org

An astounding 1,500 square miles of private land lies to the west of the 9,600-foot tabletop of Fisher's Peak, which pushes skyward on the southern Colorado horizon. The area is also home to 24,000 elk, the state's second-largest herd. Three Elk Foundation conservation easements will now forever protect 800 acres of critical wildlife habitat on the slopes of Fisher Peak.

TOP PHOTO © ERWIN AND PEGGY BAUER/WILDSTOCK.COM
BOTTOM PHOTO © DARIUS PANAHPOUR

JUNE

Nursery school: Cow elk take turns on duty watching over a small mob of calves while the others pack in the greens they need to produce copious and nutritious milk. In areas of abundant and high-quality habitat, each cow will bear a calf every spring. Where habitat is marginal, cows may only calve every other year.

SUNDAY	MONDAY	TUESDAY	WEDNESDAY	THURSDAY	FRIDAY	SATURDAY
		1	2	3	4 ◐ LAST QUARTER	5
6	7	8	9	10	11	12 ● NEW MOON
13	14 FLAG DAY	15	16	17	18	19 ◑ FIRST QUARTER
20 FATHER'S DAY	21 SUMMER SOLSTICE	22	23	24	25	26 ○ FULL MOON
27	28	29	30			

MAY 2010
						1
2	3	4	5	6	7	8
9	10	11	12	13	14	15
16	17	18	19	20	21	22
23	24	25	26	27	28	29
30	31					

JULY 2010
				1	2	3
4	5	6	7	8	9	10
11	12	13	14	15	16	17
18	19	20	21	22	23	24
25	26	27	28	29	30	31

5705 Grant Creek Road
Missoula, Montana 59808
800-CALL ELK
www.elkfoundation.org

Remnants of the Great Plains, Nebraska's Wildcat Hills shelter a burgeoning elk herd and a host of other wildlife. And thanks to a partnership between the Elk Foundation and the state, the Wildcat Hills now have 8,100 acres of new public land protected as a state wildlife management area and open to hunting.

TOP PHOTO © DAVID A. REIN
BOTTOM PHOTO © QUANG-TUAN LUONG

JULY

Mindful of their delicate velvet antlers, bulls rely on ritual posturing to telegraph dominance and submission. Come September when the velvet hardens to bone, these same bulls might fight to the death.

SUNDAY	MONDAY	TUESDAY	WEDNESDAY	THURSDAY	FRIDAY	SATURDAY
JUNE 2010 1 2 3 4 5 6 7 8 9 10 11 12 13 14 15 16 17 18 19 20 21 22 23 24 25 26 27 28 29 30	**AUGUST 2010** 1 2 3 4 5 6 7 8 9 10 11 12 13 14 15 16 17 18 19 20 21 22 23 24 25 26 27 28 29 30 31			CANADA DAY **1**	**2**	**3**
INDEPENDENCE DAY **4** ◐ LAST QUARTER	INDEPENDENCE DAY (FEDERAL HOLIDAY) **5**	**6**	**7**	**8**	**9**	**10**
11 ● NEW MOON	**12**	**13**	**14**	**15**	**16**	**17**
18 ◑ FIRST QUARTER	**19**	**20**	**21**	**22**	**23**	**24**
25 ○ FULL MOON	**26**	**27**	**28**	**29**	**30**	**31**

5705 Grant Creek Road
Missoula, Montana 59808
800-CALL ELK
www.elkfoundation.org

Lush river bottoms are a lifeline for many species in South Dakota's arid badlands. Thanks to the generosity of longtime Elk Foundation supporters, 11,128 acres encompassing the confluence of the Belle Fourche and Cheyenne rivers will offer shelter, water and prime forage and remain intact for generations to come.

TOP PHOTO © GENE PUTNEY
BOTTOM PHOTO © TOM BEAN

AUGUST

Like other subspecies, Roosevelt's elk scrape the velvet off their antlers in late August, leaving a crimson crown all the more stunning in the deep greens of the rainforest. Within hours the blood dries and the antlers whiten. Over the next several weeks, they darken to a deep brown as pigments react with oxygen and the juices of the plants on which bulls rub them.

SUNDAY	MONDAY	TUESDAY	WEDNESDAY	THURSDAY	FRIDAY	SATURDAY
1	2	3 ◐ LAST QUARTER	4	5	6	7
8	9 ● NEW MOON	10	11	12	13	14
15	16 ◑ FIRST QUARTER	17	18	19	20	21
22	23	24 ○ FULL MOON	25	26	27	28
29	30	31				

JULY 2010

				1	2	3
4	5	6	7	8	9	10
11	12	13	14	15	16	17
18	19	20	21	22	23	24
25	26	27	28	29	30	31

SEPTEMBER 2010

			1	2	3	4
5	6	7	8	9	10	11
12	13	14	15	16	17	18
19	20	21	22	23	24	25
26	27	28	29	30		

RMEF
5705 Grant Creek Road
Missoula, Montana 59808
800-CALL ELK
www.elkfoundation.org

A cattle-grazing allotment rising above Wyoming's Gros Ventre River, half the size of Teton National Park, was causing some major headaches for wildlife managers. The cattle made a serious dent in forage for elk and deer and fell prey to grizzlies and wolves. The Elk Foundation and a consortium of other groups helped retire the allotment, providing elk a valuable alternative to state-run feedgrounds.

TOP PHOTO © KEN ARCHER
BOTTOM PHOTO © TOM TOMAN

SEPTEMBER

In the frenzied heat of the September rut, bulls feel a mighty draw toward seeps and springs—the muddier the better. Such wallows cool them down, but more importantly double as a funk bath as they urinate and roll around, covering themselves in their own trademark musk.

SUNDAY	MONDAY	TUESDAY	WEDNESDAY	THURSDAY	FRIDAY	SATURDAY
AUGUST 2010 1 2 3 4 5 6 7 8 9 10 11 12 13 14 15 16 17 18 19 20 21 22 23 24 25 26 27 28 29 30 31	OCTOBER 2010 1 2 3 4 5 6 7 8 9 10 11 12 13 14 15 16 17 18 19 20 21 22 23 24 25 26 27 28 29 30 31		**1**	**2**	**3**	**4**
			◐ LAST QUARTER			
5	LABOR DAY **6**	**7**	ROSH HASHANAH BEGINS AT SUNDOWN **8** ● NEW MOON	**9**	**10**	**11**
GRANDPARENTS DAY **12**	**13**	**14**	**15** ◑ FIRST QUARTER	**16**	**17**	**18**
19	**20**	**21**	**22**	FALL EQUINOX **23** ○ FULL MOON	**24**	**25**
26	NATIONAL HUNTING AND FISHING DAY **27** YOM KIPPUR BEGINS AT SUNDOWN	**28**	**29**	**30** ◐ LAST QUARTER		

5705 Grant Creek Road
Missoula, Montana 59808
800-CALL ELK
www.elkfoundation.org

A tributary to the Snake River, Idaho's Captain John Creek provides a key spawning and rearing habitat for threatened steelhead and Chinook salmon. The Elk Foundation purchased a 160-acre inholding of crux habitat and transferred it to the Bureau of Land Management, opening it for public enjoyment as part of the 78,000-acre Craig Mountain Wildlife Management Area, home to 1,200 elk.

TOP PHOTO © GENE PUTNEY
BOTTOM PHOTO © PJ DELHOMME

OCTOBER

"I could drink that ale-golden month to its dregs and never touch a gun. But without hunting, some of the savor would be missing. I might watch game birds and animals at all seasons under a full range of conditions, and yet never know them as I do when I am hunting them well and they are doing their usual fine job of parrying my thrusts."
—John Madson, Why Men Hunt

SUNDAY	MONDAY	TUESDAY	WEDNESDAY	THURSDAY	FRIDAY	SATURDAY
SEPTEMBER 2010 　　　　1　2　3　4 5　6　7　8　9　10　11 12　13　14　15　16　17　18 19　20　21　22　23　24　25 26　27　28　29　30	NOVEMBER 2010 　1　2　3　4　5　6 7　8　9　10　11　12　13 14　15　16　17　18　19　20 21　22　23　24　25　26　27 28　29　30				1	2
3	4	5	6	7 ● NEW MOON	8	9
10	11 COLUMBUS DAY (OBSERVED) THANKSGIVING DAY (CANADA)	12	13	14 ◐ FIRST QUARTER	15	16
17	18	19	20	21	22 ○ FULL MOON	23
24	25	26	27	28	29 ◑ LAST QUARTER	30
31 HALLOWEEN						

5705 Grant Creek Road
Missoula, Montana 59808
800-CALL ELK
www.elkfoundation.org

When St. Johnswort and spotted knapweed exploded on critical winter ranges in northwest Montana's Fisher River watershed, the Elk Foundation took action, as these noxious weeds can devastate forage quality and quantity. Targeted spraying combined with weed-eating beetles help to knock back the invasive weeds so elk and other wildlife can continue to thrive.

Top Photo © Eric Ruf
Bottom Photo © Elk Foundation

NOVEMBER

"The young bull [kudu] had the start of a spiral on his horns but they were short and dumpy and as he ran past us at the end of a glade in the dusk, third in a string of six cows, he was no more like a real bull than a spike elk is like a big, old, thick-necked, dark-maned, wonder-horned, tawny-hided, beer-horse-built bugler of a bull-elk."
—Ernest Hemingway, Green Hills of Africa

SUNDAY	MONDAY	TUESDAY	WEDNESDAY	THURSDAY	FRIDAY	SATURDAY
	1	2 ELECTION DAY	3	4	5	6 ● NEW MOON
7 DAYLIGHT SAVING TIME ENDS	8	9	10	11 VETERANS DAY / REMEMBRANCE DAY (CANADA)	12	13 ◐ FIRST QUARTER
14	15	16	17	18	19	20
21 ○ FULL MOON	22	23	24	25 THANKSGIVING DAY	26	27
28 ◑ LAST QUARTER	29	30			OCTOBER 2010	DECEMBER 2010

OCTOBER 2010
					1	2
3	4	5	6	7	8	9
10	11	12	13	14	15	16
17	18	19	20	21	22	23
24	25	26	27	28	29	30
31

DECEMBER 2010
			1	2	3	4
5	6	7	8	9	10	11
12	13	14	15	16	17	18
19	20	21	22	23	24	25
26	27	28	29	30	31

5705 Grant Creek Road
Missoula, Montana 59808
800-CALL ELK
www.elkfoundation.org

An unwavering troop of conifers was marching on Oregon's Grasshopper Meadow. With years of fire suppression, the trees faced little opposition as they invaded the elk's grassy oasis. Stepping into the skirmish, the Elk Foundation helped slash small-diameter trees, set fire to 147 acres, and reseed 104 of them with nutritious native grasses.

TOP PHOTO © MARK LAGERSTROM
BOTTOM PHOTO © ELK FOUNDATION

DECEMBER

In winter, most cows are doing the double-work of carrying next spring's calves in their wombs. Times are lean, but that isn't all that bad. A fat cow is a slow cow, and when running from predators, slow cows lose.

SUNDAY	MONDAY	TUESDAY	WEDNESDAY	THURSDAY	FRIDAY	SATURDAY
NOVEMBER 2010 1 2 3 4 5 6 7 8 9 10 11 12 13 14 15 16 17 18 19 20 21 22 23 24 25 26 27 28 29 30	JANUARY 2011 1 2 3 4 5 6 7 8 9 10 11 12 13 14 15 16 17 18 19 20 21 22 23 24 25 26 27 28 29 30 31		HANUKKAH BEGINS AT SUNDOWN **1**	**2**	**3**	**4**
5 ● NEW MOON	**6**	**7**	**8**	**9**	**10**	**11**
12	**13** ◐ FIRST QUARTER	**14**	**15**	**16**	**17**	**18**
19	**20**	WINTER SOLSTICE **21** ○ FULL MOON	**22**	**23**	**24**	CHRISTMAS DAY **25**
BOXING DAY (CANADA) **26**	**27** ◑ LAST QUARTER	**28**	**29**	**30**	**31**	

5705 Grant Creek Road
Missoula, Montana 59808
800-CALL ELK
www.elkfoundation.org

As development accelerates in Oregon's Wallowa Valley, two longtime Elk Foundation supporters donated a 678-acre conservation easement that lies less than three miles from the Eagle Cap Wilderness. The easement protects critical winter range for mule deer and a year-round habitat for elk—as many as 300 at a time.

TOP PHOTO © NELSON KENTER
BOTTOM PHOTO © PJ DELHOMME

THE MISSION OF THE ROCKY MOUNTAIN ELK FOUNDATION IS TO ENSURE THE FUTURE OF ELK, OTHER WILDLIFE AND THEIR HABITAT.

Published in cooperation with *Bugle* magazine and the Rocky Mountain Elk Foundation.

For more information, (800) CALL-ELK or visit us at www.elkfoundation.org.

5705 Grant Creek Road
Missoula, Montana 59808
800-CALL ELK
www.elkfoundation.org

US $9.95 / CAN $11.95
ISBN 978-1-59921-554-9

THE LYONS PRESS
Guilford, Connecticut
The Lyons Press is an imprint of
The Globe Pequot Press

For additional copies of this calendar, please check with your local bookstore, or to order by phone, call toll-free (800) 243-0495.

Visit our Web site at www.LyonsPress.com.
Copyright © 2009 Morris Book Publishing, LLC
Printed in China

Cover photo © Ken Archer
Inside front cover photo © donaldmjones.com